CREEPY CRAWLIES

Centipedes

by Kari Schuetz

BLASTOFF!
READERS

Note to Librarians, Teachers, and Parents:

Blastoff! Readers are carefully developed by literacy experts and combine standards-based content with developmentally appropriate text.

Level 1 provides the most support through repetition of high-frequency words, light text, predictable sentence patterns, and strong visual support.

Level 2 offers early readers a bit more challenge through varied simple sentences, increased text load, and less repetition of high-frequency words.

Level 3 advances early-fluent readers toward fluency through increased text and concept load, less reliance on visuals, longer sentences, and more literary language.

Level 4 builds reading stamina by providing more text per page, increased use of punctuation, greater variation in sentence patterns, and increasingly challenging vocabulary.

Level 5 encourages children to move from "learning to read" to "reading to learn" by providing even more text, varied writing styles, and less familiar topics.

Whichever book is right for your reader, Blastoff! Readers are the perfect books to build confidence and encourage a love of reading that will last a lifetime!

This edition first published in 2016 by Bellwether Media, Inc.

No part of this publication may be reproduced in whole or in part without written permission of the publisher. For information regarding permission, write to Bellwether Media, Inc., Attention: Permissions Department, 5357 Penn Avenue South, Minneapolis, MN 55419.

Library of Congress Cataloging-in-Publication Data

Schuetz, Kari, author.
  Centipedes / by Kari Schuetz.
     pages cm. – (Blastoff! Readers. Creepy Crawlies)
  Summary: "Developed by literacy experts for students in kindergarten through grade three, this book introduces centipedes to young readers through leveled text and related photos"– Provided by publisher.
  Audience: Ages 5-8
  Audience: K to grade 3
  Includes bibliographical references and index.
  ISBN 978-1-62617-221-0 (hardcover: alk. paper)
  1. Centipedes–Juvenile literature. I. Title.
  QL449.5.S38 2016
  595.6′2–dc23
                              2015002647

Printed in the United States of America, North Mankato, MN.

Table of **Contents**

Lots of Legs   4

Deadly Claws   8

A Life in Hiding   14

So Many Eggs   18

Glossary   22

To Learn More   23

Index   24

Lots of Legs

Centipedes are speedy **arthropods**. They have long **antennae** and many legs.

4

antennae

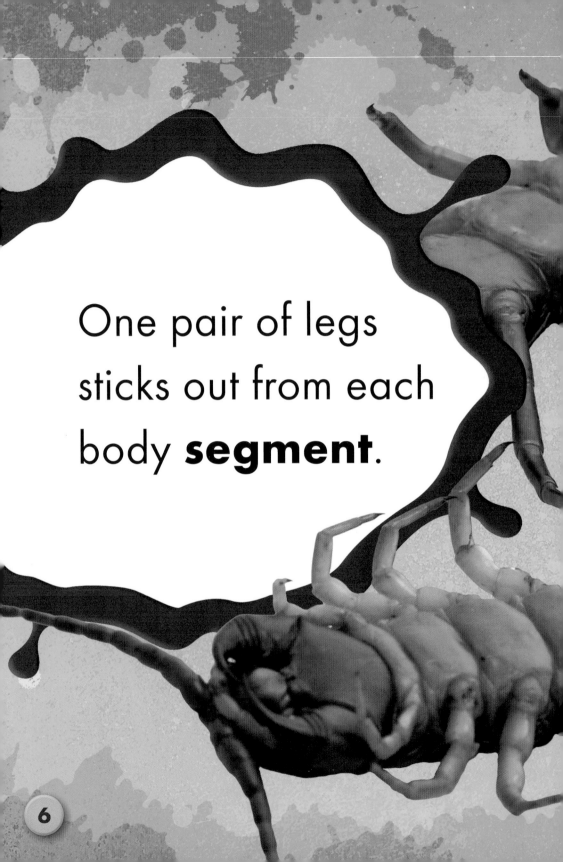

One pair of legs sticks out from each body **segment**.

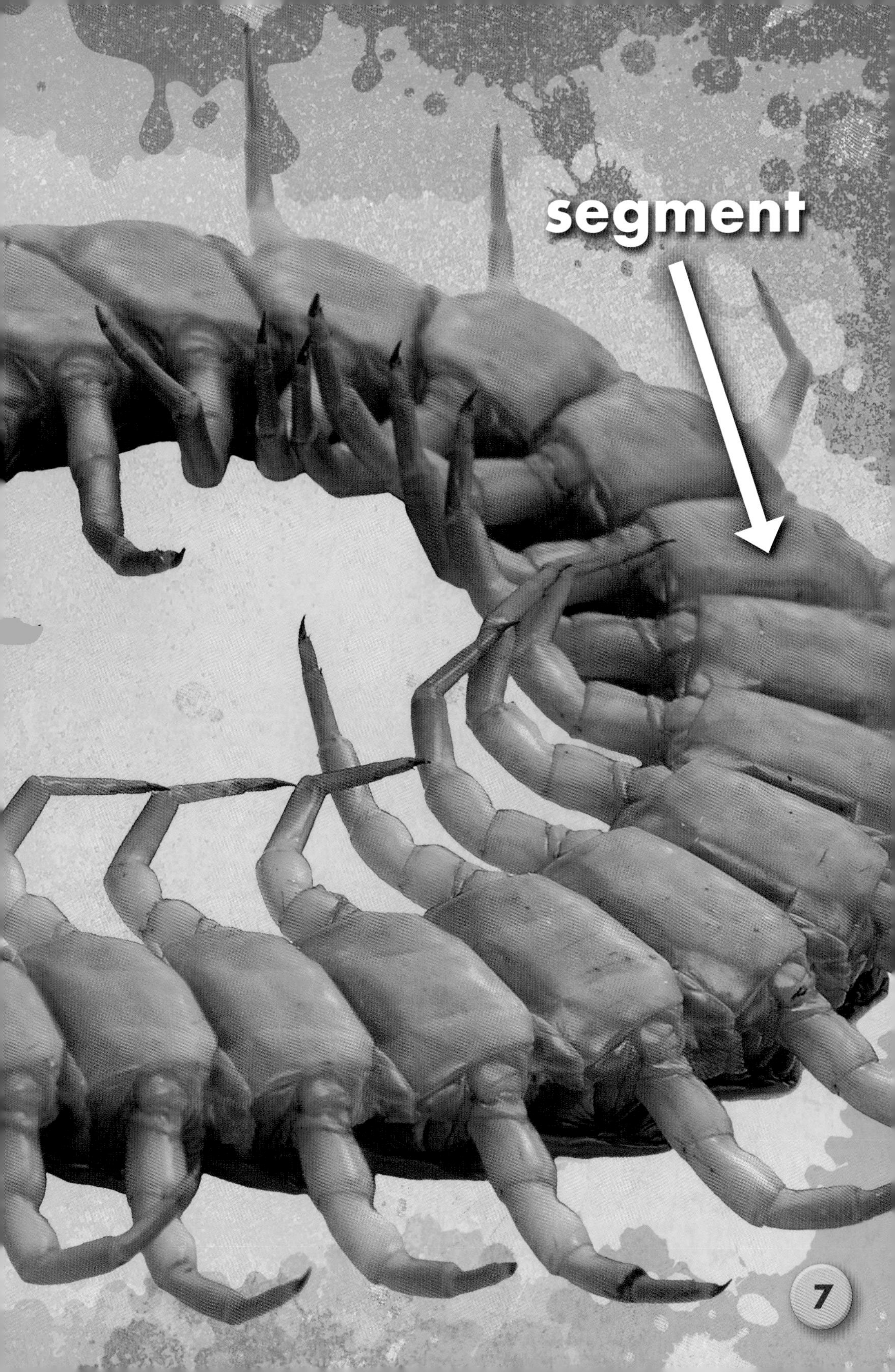
segment

Deadly Claws

Two legs behind
the head act
like claws. They
shoot **venom**
into **prey**.

9

Insects, spiders, and worms must be careful. The venom can **paralyze**.

Then the
helpless prey
becomes dinner!

A Life in Hiding

Centipedes like to stay in **damp**, dark places.

They hide under rocks, leaves, and logs during the day. Then they hunt at night.

So Many Eggs

Females lay a **clutch** of about 60 eggs. The eggs often stick together.

Most females bury their eggs in soil. Soon the babies **hatch**. Time to move!

Glossary

antennae–feelers connected to the head

arthropods–small animals, such as insects and spiders, that have divided bodies

clutch–a group of eggs

damp–a little bit wet

hatch–to break out of an egg

insects–small animals with six legs and hard outer bodies; an insect's body is divided into three parts.

paralyze–to stop the movement of something

prey–animals that are hunted by other animals for food

segment–a part or division

venom–a poison

To Learn More

AT THE LIBRARY

Bodden, Valerie. *Centipedes*. Mankato, Minn.:
Creative Education, 2011.

Rissman, Rebecca. *Centipedes*. Chicago, Ill.:
Raintree, 2013.

Ross, Tony. *Centipede's 100 Shoes*. New
York, N.Y.: H. Holt, 2003.

ON THE WEB

Learning more about
centipedes is as easy
as 1, 2, 3.

1. Go to www.factsurfer.com.

2. Enter "centipedes" into the search box.

3. Click the "Surf" button and you will see a
   list of related web sites.

With factsurfer.com, finding more information
is just a click away.

Index

antennae, 4, 5
arthropods, 4
bury, 20
claws, 8
clutch, 18
damp, 14
dark, 14
day, 16
eggs, 18, 20
females, 18, 20
hatch, 20
head, 8
hide, 16
hunt, 16
insects, 10
leaves, 16

legs, 4, 6, 8
logs, 16
night, 16
paralyze, 10
prey, 8, 12
rocks, 16
segment, 6, 7
soil, 20
speedy, 4
spiders, 10
venom, 8, 10
worms, 10

The images in this book are reproduced through the courtesy of: THPStock, front cover; Audrey Snider-Bell, pp. 5, 17; PanStock, p. 7; Nicky Bay/ National Geographic Creative/ Corbis, p. 9; thanom, p. 11 (centipede); Henrik Larsson, p. 11 (spider); Larry Miller/ Science Source, p. 13; CPbackpacker, p. 15; Wild & Natural/ Age Fotostock, p. 19; Carol Hughes/ Gallo Images/ Corbis, p. 21.